Academy of the Supernatural

Also by Rory Steele
Obverse & Parallel Lines

Rory Steele

Academy of the Superfluous

John

in admiration and with affection.

Rory

February 2006

GINNINDERRA PRESS

Acknowledgements

Some of these poems have been previously published:
'Developing Zoo Solutions', *Quadrant*, 2002; 'Visit to the National Gallery',
Quadrant, 1984; 'What Went on in Einstein's Head, Ordinarily?', *Quadrant*,
1980; 'The Clock Collector', *Quadrant*, 1983; 'Mummybeads', *Quadrant*, 1984;
'The Villa of Mysteries', *Quadrant*, 1987; 'Off Broadway', *Poetry Australia*,
1991; 'Rothko Opera', *Quadrant*, 1986; 'London Ladies Dancing', *Quadrant*,
1991; 'Roundheads 3, Cavaliers 0', *Quadrant*, 1993; 'Strange Rites Near Tring',
Quadrant, 1986; 'Toast to Grotefend', *Quadrant*, 1988; 'The Cutting Edge',
Quadrant, 1984; 'Oral Histories', *Quadrant*, 1989; 'Precarious', *Quadrant*, 1986;
'Running Out', *Quadrant*, 1987; 'Giddy Down', *Westerly*, 1985; 'Balanced
Horror Diet', *Quadrant*, 1985, & *Australian Poetry*, 1986; 'Remember How
We Will Be Children', *Westerly*, 1987; 'Graffiti Paradox', *Quadrant*, 1989;
'Frog From', *Quadrant*, 1990; 'Daydream', *Quadrant*, 1986; 'Rockfight at
Maralunga', *Westerly*, 1983; 'Umbrian Museum Horror', *Meanjin*, 2000;
'Agostin O Pazz', *Quadrant*, 1987, & *Australian Poetry*, 1988; 'Incident in
Sicily', *Quadrant*, 1987; 'flying.monk@copertino', *Quadrant*, 2000; 'Athens
Hospital', *Southerly*, 1990; 'Gibraltar Glory', *Hobo*, 1998; 'At Thebes', *Westerly*,
1988; 'Outremer', *Quadrant*, 1985; 'Home Via Darwin', *Quadrant*, 1986;
'Cladding 1988', *Southerly*, 1989; 'Hunter Valley Camouflage', *Quadrant*, 1985;
'SS At Adelong', *Quadrant*, 1989; 'The Crow and the Baby', *Westerly*, 1987;
'March 1918: Orders To His Men', *Sydney Review*, 1988; 'King's Revenge',
Quadrant, 1993; 'Peeking', *Quadrant*, 1985; 'The Garden Path', *Quadrant*, 1984;
'Trial and Error', *Quadrant*, 1984; 'Crossing', *Quadrant*, 1985; 'Vulgar and Vain
Fractions', *Quadrant*, 1984; 'Anachronisms', *Quadrant*, 1985; 'Improbability',
Westerly, 1983; 'Suspension', *Quadrant*, 1984; 'Or', *Quadrant*, 1982; 'No Smell
Museum', *Southerly*, 1990; 'Of Parabolas and Parables', *Quadrant*, 1982; 'Real
Time', *Southerly*, 1985; 'Hard Words and Lullabies', *Westerly*, 1985; 'Ancientest
Power', *Quadrant*, 1988; 'You Like a Good Murder', *Quadrant*, 1990; 'Don't
Overegg', *Quadrant*, 1990; 'Pilate's Question', *Quadrant*, 1984; 'It Can't
Happen To Me', *Westerly*, 1994; 'The Last', *Quadrant*, 2000.

Academy of the Superfluous
ISBN 1 74027 324 9
Copyright © Rory Steele 2006

First published in this form 2006 by
GINNINDERRA PRESS
PO Box 6753 Charnwood ACT 2615
www.ginninderrapress.com.au

Printed by Pirion Digital, Fyshwick, ACT

Contents

Developing Zoo Solutions

Trapezoidal roof and verandas silhouetted
Against the sky suggest the head of a giraffe.
Instead it's an elegant wood queenslander gazetted
To go – out of its place, the shapes here all
Right-angled perpendiculars, blocks of flats looming
On a knoll above Brisbane, ideas mushrooming,
Turning to concrete and glass developers' tall
Stories, their pride in prices bound never to fall.
You can sense the machine of mad safari guns booming,
The knell of earthmovers in nestling gums dooming
Numberless old architectural creatures great and small.
Zoo-like compromises, however, might make you laugh:
This beauty can be moved somewhere nice, unregretted,
Unendangered, easy – it just gets first sawn in half.

Visit to the National Gallery

Heads are like new-fangled boxes, stacked deliberately
With odds and ends – mirrors, tangled strings, and eyes –
Mine peer, detached, set back inside behind their frame
At angled collar, elbow, programme-holding hand;
Impressions linger on the face, just out of sight,
Reflected in third-party posturings. 'What
Pollock meant…' as though his head was on display revealing
Strands of anger, doubt, exuberance, securely tied;
Of course a real painter may have single themes,
Not be alarmingly detached like me. And proper critics
With their index fingers have no trouble tracing lines
While dinkum highwaymen might range the bush, quite witting
In the dramas they must act before they hang.
Masks are messages, messages and masks belong
In hollow halls. It's closing time. I knot my tie
Vainly in revolving glass, and step outside.

What Went On In Einstein's Head, Ordinarily?

Everyman dreams he's extraordinary
Such analysis is proof enough.
Wheatfields of the mind extend
Ripe and yellow, end to end
Ear to ear, deadly flat.
In the mirror just awake
I rake the stubble with the back
Of a nailbit hand and think
Of peasants with their right-size plots
Scything sheaves and heaving sighs
Backs cry quietly to ease the curve.

Only tractors and vast machinery
Track across my waving thoughts;
If I could squat against a stook
And chew a stalk and watch ants walk
Things less ordinary might…
Might what? I shrug. Might germinate.

The Honeyed Cat

I'm upside down back to front
you you are gone
sucking black holes
between ears behind eyes
time a tar gum yoyo
drawls zips away.

Riffled snaps of you drawerfuls
testing me now I guess then
here neat Gioconda dwarfed
by the piazza
and a huge bronze horse.

Men are such simple dogs.
Women, felines – awe
of fur, claw, depths, beauty and disdain;
you adored from the first,
honey-haired enigma
beyond metaphor.

Like cats in calendars of Rome
drawing the eye from looming
vastnesses of marble
you trounce Donatello's
Gattamelata outside
the basilica in Padua;

bronze bounds on the pedestal
but giddy from reverie
you are the warrior
your clouds boil
your golden light bursts
while I am the figurine

the traveller blessing St
Anthony for holy discoveries
so glad that I found you
glad I was found.

The Clock Collector

Near-meticulous my love
Like a clock collector
Seconds tick correct
But inexactly synchronised
Very striking
Dustless place, particular
But cluttered bookcases
Characteristically
Smoke-choked ashtrays

Time for me unregulated
Sets in moons and moods
Alarms forget so
Daybreak cocks don't doodle
Each watch unshowerproof
Shaving mirror mesmerised
Reflects a sprinting train

Ormolu love
We click we talk you
Save me time
And time again

Hard Words and Lullabies

Cribs, cots, cradles rock like seas
Like hammocks crescented in Cs
Sinecures and fantasies
How here on in it starts to ease
At halfway-marking-time
Paces downhill stretch or shrink
To come to terms

But come oh darling come to bed
No compromise now in this word
Bad nightmares of the long long wed
Arguments too often heard
Bones on boards, stone steps ahead
Time concertinas, big jobs bid
On their own terms

Mummybeads

Strings of
Bright coincidences
Link us like talking points
Among acquaintances – how did you two meet?
Oh, it started when he tore a ligament
And then in hospital
Thanks to this

Thanks to robbers
Hacking dark at crumbly wood
Linen bandages, broad beaded collars ripped aside
For diadems, gold, pectorals of lapis lazuli
Cheaper tributes strewn in sand
Along the dynasties
Not traced

Till Sunday
Head down point-blank scavenging
On all fours, bums up in the air
We scanned Sakkara's desert floor that afternoon
Sifting a necropolis for tiny beads
Four thousand years old perhaps
Got thirty-eight

Creating starts
In darkness, mucking round with
Hieroglyphic thoughts at first and wonders
Subsequent revealed. Under the sun
There may be nothing new perhaps
So what

About these thoughts
They slip as sand between fingers
Timegrains in a pharaoh's hourglass
Gembits picked out chuckling strung
On catgut roughly knotted
Poetry for you

The Villa of Mysteries

In the Villa of Mysteries we slip-rope a door
Down an umbra of steps to a cellar below
Dark, forgotten; thin steles of sunlight won't show
Where we huddle each other in dust on the floor.
Up there tourists pose with their cameras, restore
Form to the inchoate, snap status quo
Onto jumbles of ruins; but buses must go.
Ghosts take the stage then, alone, as before.
Performances, lines learned from guidebooks, rehearsed
Histories; thus passing years replenish
The carbons that flamed in full life then dispersed.
Go back? Oh, how might not these years diminish
That date…unless, one red second could burst
Astonishing, fixing for ever, then vanish.

Academy of the Superfluous

We've had oiled madonnas and crucifixions
up to here, soaked up more culture than a sponge
then dog-tired as Romans do take the plunge
into homicidal traffic scantly regarding restrictions
and police. Over life-saving coffee we make our confessions:
bodies also need food and species have their urge
for sex while money is today's absolute scourge
and, shit, now someone just stole our worldly possessions
namely, tickets, passports and plastic. We seek directions
to the consulate where we have got to report
and en route in a street with baroque contradictions,
the weirdest-sounding academy and outrageously smart
passers-by, ask just what are its functions?
One smiles forgivingly. Oh, they teach art.

Off Broadway

Here they live elevated and apartmented
Dense ad libbed lives
And the sidewalks, blocks gridded
Are boxed like shows
Everybody's cast
No wonder the dramas enacted
Under the street lights
Of 41st and 5th
A quartet apart declaiming
Peak-capped labelled SULLIVAN;
Lady, do you mean that?
Driver, offended, goes into attack
Middle-aged black man moves back
Bystander angry with shopping bags
Claims a main role
Theft, knockdown, badly parked?
Eyes hood in the halflight
Palms sweep unheard words
Roles seem to switch
Black man mocks
Bystander nods
Cop arms akimbo
She with the keys stands shocked
A one-man audience
I exit
Check my ticket
Beware of pickpockets
Must rush
To the real theatre

Rothko Opera

For me? A bath of red paint upended,
One dark swab swished thick with a
Hard yard broom. I see no sense.

Michelangelo dissects a tracery of sinews;
Behind pen-nib lens and fine-wire nerve
Lies sight, however, washed in red veils,
Which alarm clocks rend yellow at daybreak;
Officeworkers unblinded at lunchtime,
Rubber drums rumble in Midtown,
Orchestras honk, screech and sink sounding;
Ears under water hum and guess voices.
Imagine a bath full of French perfume,
Outrageously spilled and the headrush depicted,
Abstracted chiaro in scent-swamped oscuro.

Canned Laughter – Orlando, Fla

Near the rentacar ignition key a Message Center
Brings up data and instructions – Fasten Belt, Low Fuel –
Such conveniences are overly adequate.

Highway billboards, two-dimension structures, advocate
Tabloid puns; selected eye-dilating colors market
Tomato red and mustard gold. At night these merge.

Readily digested fast food menus: adjectives
Splurge like catsup, 'farmfresh fluffy omelet,
Coffee piping hot'. Lyrical maple syrup.

Motel air-conditioning camouflages other sounds
But not adjacent prime-time TV comedies;
Canned laughter punctuates each second line.

I could add this up and moralise for you,
Pay attention, we are being programmed!
(Exclamation mark a cue to titter, shortly.)

London Ladies Dancing

Furred Chelsea lady, you dancing
At your age by parked cars, red letter box,
Or crippled, St. Vitus…? Ah, no, rather
A soft shoe-shit shuffle, she stops now
Mid-pavement to scrape.

High wind in Hyde Park, pale sunshine,
A black-brollied matron diagonal
Billowed and tacking on tiptoe
Foot-lifted comes happily singing.
The dog-walkers dodge.

Office girls skip in the Underground.
Exploits near Leicester Square, fair sex
Cavorting, some decent; the dirty old
Buildings transvested in neons,
And all London dances.

Roundheads 3, Cavaliers 0

Hundreds of years since Edgehill & Marston Moor
Charlie, and we're still at it
Tromping around Worcestershire
Waiting to engage: kick-off due at 3 p.m.
Our musketeers are holed out in the pub
With their drummer-boy wives and girlfriends.
Caravans like baggage trains parked round the back
Disgorge the newly-changed in smock and breeches;
Cannon are unloaded from a hired truck
By yeomen bankers and real estate agents.
You and me, Charlie, officers and bookmakers,
Not spoiling for the fight as much as urged
Like them by the universal lust for dressing up.
I don't know how pleased Oliver Cromwell
Would be at all this achieved egalitarianism.

At last a little after quarter to
The fifes and pennants form in line with
Cavalry from the local pony club
Plumed and snorting on the flank;
Over from Germany a troop of skirmishers
Just revelling in the reenactment,
And then it's on. Clumps of rugby men
With 16-foot pikes slowly mesh together
Like great mating hedgehogs in several scrums,
Leather heels pedalling in soggy grass.
There's a clear risk of broken ribs and noses,
With mock or real gore on gorgeous silk.
Game, spectacle, film-set; an amplified voice
Elaborately directs levels of reality
For day-out families behind the barriers
Where knots of tourist camaramen aim and fire;
You could conclude we're surfeiting with peace,
For nearly fifty years without a proper war
Is doing strange things to us, Charlie.

Strange Rites, Near Tring

Hertfordshire papyrus reeds good for thatch
Ripple along the canal where mummies crouch
Swaddled, age-frozen, hoping for the touch
Of Ra to reel through their veins and rush
Them. A rooster practises against the hush.
From time to time the surface tension pops, fresh
Silver writhed parabolas whose fate is mesh
Basketry at waterlevel, for the catch.
When it's time to go they're all tossed back: I wish
I knew what for. An angler makes a speech
About life and continuity; look they splash
Off happily as anything. But don't they mind the gash
That signals certain death? We peer at each
Other uncomprehendingly. You should ask the fish.

I Can Hardly See

I can hardly picture Warsaw flat:
Its chorusing churches look old
While the new-leaved trees
Loom like giants in the parks,
Can't wrap my mind around
The ordered disorder –
First torch then dynamite
Each house, film and file this,
Rubble not to reach knee-high,
Every living soul to be
Displaced or entombed.
Eight hundred thousand died.

Modern shops sprout the way
They do, and just unveiled
A lumping bronze monument
Of huge rat-wild men
Emerging from the drains;
Today small clustered girls
Guided by a seeing nun
Meet the first man out
In dazzling slants of light,
Must feel with sliding hands
The cold rag folds and one
By one on pointing toes hope
To find the blazed eyes;
None of those watching can speak.

Later I think of my photographs
Taken shakily, still dark-boxed,
Waiting for their time to blink.

Toast to Grotefend

Grotefend read the first writing for a bet
Made boozing with his mates in Gottingen
He said, I'll tell that gibberish in cuneiform
Chiselled in the tablets of Persepolis;
Harsh German Ach-du-Lehrer! belly laughs.

Schoolmaster's beer-bubbles disappear
To outer space where good thoughts drift
At edge of eye a sungleam winks
An unfound star must be – it is!

For the record, Flood and Ark were
Scooped in the first tale of Gilgamesh
And Hammurabi's legal code predates
Israel's plaint in Babylon.
He won his bet.

Wedge-shaped scalpels maybe cut between
Grotefend's thunderdark ganglia
Let lightning in – king, son of king
Xerxes bursts from the insoluble.

Bubbles blip in sun, well, drink to this:
Our thoughts fill vast dull libraries
Not anyway decipherable.
But genius, two lines in tomes,
That's all, one sip worth thirsting for.

The Cutting Edge

The ink could well be dry before I end the line
To contradict reporting in the present tense;
But it's about the past and future that I write.
As tourists dulled by cobblestones these thoughts of mine
Protest the Palais de Justice's dungeons, whence
Aristos are being led in groups of twelve, in white
Rough rags up dragging steps; and cocky warders shine
With actuality at vileness to commence,
At violence for change, for good. Drum, tambourine
Are dinning individual signals to each spine
That this must cut and end; the craning mobs can sense
The thrill of continuity in their machine.

By chance the Paris Marathon is on today.
Spectators congregate in Place de la Concorde;
In bunches thirteen thousand runners from the right
Appear, red poppy singlets blink against the grey.
Perversely dazed with Michelin Guide I make this horde
Come streaming through in '93, and out of sight.
The Romans may have had massed games right here and they
Were civilised, reformist, excellent; adored
Odd gods for whom grand public deaths were not obscene.
Benign we jog for human rights, and who's to say
This leads to excellence? Democracy restored
But dawdling: excellence may race the guillotine.

Oral Histories

There was this joke-teller
Who with wicked, slick,
Quick-as-Picasso
Cameos misrepresented life
Recognisably, had us in creases:
You envied his repertoire,
Deftness in this most
Portable artform.
You know we've our gallery
Of memorable anecdotes
Sketched and resketched
Fixtures adorning the walls
Of our years.
You can embellish them,
Fuzz edges, shift colour –
Friends puzzle a little,
But words are like brushes
Dipped in impermanence,
Like everything naturally.
There's something to be said
For such histories,
Possibly.

Precarious

God teeters and freezes
Top tightrope walker
Unencumbered by gender or number
Balance is perfect
Earth spins serenely
Though weather turns turtle
And all else seems random
You hold your breath, wonder
Will I keel over?
Crave as a favour
Rightness
I favour
Chewing left side
Sleeping left side
I write right
Am odd and distorted
People in the street
Eyes lined with the horizon
Twist and limp though it hurts
To keep even
Bodies
Never mind minds

Running Out

Come back with something duty-free
Aunt Mary said, the widow's cruse
Runs out, you know, except in parables.

Down there men can in hand
Have left their cars beside the road
To trudge for oil or something else
That is like them adaptable;
Lifelong forests, see, capitulate
In concrete fields, wilderness is dammed
Erosion's duller coloured uniforms
Advance in dunes and factories
Towards the wen, ah, clouds shroud it all.

I don't know if I will go back.
The cramped and yelling flat
Would probably adjust to this quite soon,
Quite well.

Things aren't so durable
These days.

Giddy Down

Smoke, noise, no, I don't remember these
But clearly see the heads or tails
In steelwheel minted pennies on the track
Below our house: we'd wait for trains
Chance madly down the bank and squealing back.

We moved that year to somewhere middler class
And with shifts in time improved on that address
In upward social spiralling. From here
I see my kids have never walked on rails
But out of sight they must have plunged in fear.

It's giddy-making looking down from planes
Or high-rise buildings at the mess
Of have-not mediocrity, delayed
By accident of time in shock which sees
Recurring dreams of Railway Parade.

Balanced Horror Diet

Kidneys, liver, spinach made me scream
To eat, with shrill entreaties these were 'Good
For You!' Such vileness fortified the blood,
Allegedly. A yell can let off steam
And that's not bad. The odd horrific dream
Evens out in daytime as the flood
Of fantasies is dammed and understood
And channelled down some safe and conscious stream.
Children maybe need to feel real fear
To get things in perspective, to ignore
The routine dread; so bogeymen appear
In Grimm's gross shapes – though nowadays they're more
Boxed and processed, fast-food violence, near
As screens, blurbed urban gun-deaths, ketchup gore.

Remember How We Will Be Children

Remember how we will be children
Nursery years ahead;
The big printed books that taught us to read
Help us to unlearn instead
Continence, arrogance, freedom to speak
All you want. The weak
Watch where they tread.

Spring is snug in the black buds of winter,
Time's grandparent tense,
But tomorrow for old men and babies
Makes little sense.
Good old days, simple times, hanker these back,
They were grim; and smack
Of mental defence.

Today in the full fledge of science
Those long in the tooth
Can with plastic and chips and new organs
Get back bits of youth;
Ordinary miracles, nothing too strange
Or impossible: now change
May synthesise truth.

In playgrounds first lessons in chaos,
Brutes sort of conform;
In a dark hall the seniors assemble,
Ephemeral fads then perform;
Sundown clouds clamber as night starts to fall;
Who wants to recall
The probable storm?

Graffiti Paradox

Red paint soaks into brick's
Sticky bed. Get that off.
Maddened powers grab some kid
Who, drubbed, must scrub with kerosene
And make a filthy mess of Ks
That kicked, Rs marching, double E
Now with broken teeth.
The writing, yes, was on the wall
The space still calls
For its message. You hear mumbling
In bus queues, the word is out. Odd:
If it needs to be said
It need not be said
And vice versa.
The writer knows they should also
Hate the space.

The Sniper

God delights in symmetry
the pebbles in the pond are yours
the rings are his
toylike rippling out
he sits above the tennis courts
juggles the departure times
and from four parts of town
the players then converge
to pepper a white molecule
a dense and frenzied hour
and centrifuge
the public courts were full that day
he must have scried
an interlocking intricately
patterned web
mad spiders in the dew

The tennis court down there is bare
few wisps of smoke
below me four roads meet
I sit a bit like God
the life of all that moves beneath
depends on me
in sometime bursts of energy
I pepper molecules of lead about
but windows eat them up
and once or twice
a target staggers
angularly out of sight
wouldn't it be nice to know
where every single bullet goes?
God guards this secret
what you would expect
but balance
balance guards he best of all

Frog From

Not.
Gone.
Join the dots up.
Turn the fan on.
Whirr you here
I wish

Jogged once
Drought just broken
Got croaked at
Soggy grassclumps
Jump, hey, where you
Frog from?

I squat
Crossleg yogaman
Bake my mind
Dry as a creek bed
Less hot before breakfast
Stand on my head
Thoughtless

Then you hop
Sun spotted emerald
Down on my lilypad
Membrane brain
Startling choruses
Chortling remember
Pondsplash

I pour grog
Get a frog
In my throat sometimes

Daydream

In fact
Nothing occurred.
Night by night
I rehearsed, was word
Perfect, gestures right,
Schemed the best time
For this act,
For this mime!
When the chance came
It skipped in dumb dance;
But in daylight's
Real dreams
Same things play
To a different script.

Rockfight at Maralunga di Lerici

We were killing lizards with our slingshots
Fausto five, me four and Vito two
Splatter slivers of grey and green quicksilver
On the rockface among the prickly pears.
There's a shout 'Come on quick, a gang from town!'
And five small boys run up in full alarm.
'Nascondi la fionda,' hide the slingshot,
Says Vito, 'we'll do better chucking rocks.'
They challenged, we choose weapons, which is easy
On a dirt road thick with powdered dust
Countless stones the size of children's fists.
They have slope and numbers in their favour
Quickly force us back to the pine grove park
And the first shots rain through flimsy cover
Gathered, hurled back up for both sides see
There are no rocks on the sand-and-needle floor.
'The churchyard!' then a fifty-metre gallop
Down steps to a stucco barricade
Walling in a small and sullen chapel;
Soon heaven showers missiles to this sanctum,
One passes by my face as I peer upwards,
For the moment we're quite safe, but well trapped.
Fausto, Vito, several of us jump down
Through the olive orchard hidden at the side,
Creep in the lee of retaining terrace walls
Up through the trees to the road by the pines.
They've seen us too soon! No, too late for them
Now they're attacked from two directions,
One casualty each, thirty near misses;
But the end comes fast: 'Curse you wretches!'
It's Fausto's father. 'Rocks in my house!
Will you kill someone!' He chases the foe;
Like wind in the olives our gang melts away.

Umbrian Museum Horror

It's like old socks and sneakers peeking out to spoil
the fancy gown: those ads and petrol stations coil
along the plain, while grey-green olives gently curve
up to the gemmed and clustered turret-towns observing
safer from malaria and wars the undulating soil
whose crop transfuses under granite wheels to golden oil.

Convert a church – a museum that will take its place
unearths a chute of corpses tossed from grace
and sudden nineteenth century plague all preserved
miraculously with clothes, teeth, skin and hair,
a booted fusilier, a friar's leathered face,
two little girls whose wrists are sheathed with lace.

If their eyes were now to flick awake they'd be appalled
to see steel beams, double glaze, the razor-cornered wall;
if they levered up on elbow, might meet some tourist's stare;
and if they tottered to the door and gazed below despairing,
would shriek at factories, cement, the autostrada's scrawl,
at Umbria sprayed, painted, pyloned, the ghastly sprawl.

Smoke, Fire

Black conclave smoke might have puffed in Dante's day
on and on until at last a compromise: the holy man
high in the Apennines saw winding up a pageant,
cardinals caparisoned, his strangest vision yet;
he took the papal name of Celestine the Fifth.

History is a scene of arson and we must sift for clues.
It seems the hermit was a hopeless pope, unfailingly
granted each request, no sense of politics, stoked
factions inadvertently, was outmanoeuvred and replaced
by Boniface – whom Dante thrust amid the flames of hell.

Fumone, which means big smoke, is a hill-top citadel
whose role had always been to warn of threats to Rome;
in its massy fastnesses Celestine was locked away,
his cell just over coffin-length and not a metre wide;
food was passed in through a narrow aperture.

He survived one winter there and died aged 81.
Some say his successor wanted him to be immured
but that a fiery cross appeared outside the cell.
The only pope to ever abdicate was made a saint
in less than twenty years – just why, it's hard to tell.

Agostin O Pazz

Black cockaded stallions clop
Through cobbled backstreets
With their hearse behind bedecked
In arum lilies, arabesques and curling scrolls;
Family mourners sheepish trail
And pseudo-sombre raggle-taggle
Queues of curious swell the rear;
In Via Roma mocha coffee wafts with
Aromatic fumes of fuel and cooking
From flats above small shops;
The shoppers stop to see a funeral
Proceed and men salute with
Hand to head for grace of God
And genuflexive reverence.

Then crescendo thunder
Up the street illegally against the flow
Of metal drums and cymbals
Hammered mad, a
Huddled motorbike
That checks, rears, screeches
Off through pavement tables
Down a basket-selling alley
Ululates towards the port.

The mob soul-jolted sighs instinctive
'Agostin o pazz!' and many smile.

The madman kept at large like this for months
Till caught, locked up, and freed at last;
To star in films of Agostin. which roared
On screens in Pòrtici and Vòmero.

Incident in Sicily

Eyewitnesses cross themselves and lie
Round-mouthed, photographed in the lit lunacy
Of judgement night, glazed red and cream by turns,
Sirens keening.
The mayor glimpsed amid milling villagers, cries
In the road, still things, made by God or man,
Lose meaning.
The driver, perhaps come round to Hell,
Backs from the shawls, the eyes, the law
Shrugging.
An unscathed donkey bursts its lungs.

flying.monk@copertino

Joe – this is a dead dull town down at the heel
of Italy, just a hop and a skip from Brindisi.
Streetsigns for your natal saint are pure cartoon – a smiling
haloed catapulted apteryx in robes –

thither the stable where he was born, impeccable credentials.
Seems St Joseph was a real dunce at school. Flukily, the
exam for the seminary
set the only text he'd ever memorised.

But could he fly! He'd shoot up in ecstasy
(no innuendoes) to ceilings, to treetop height,
took friends along all this is documented.
He flew at court, over crowds, sensationally.

Pope Urban the Eighth witnessed it, furious.
So what is weirder: that Joe defied every known law, or
instead that we shrug the achievement off?
Ask your students: he's their patron saint, after all.

Athens Hospital

DIAGNOSIS AND THERAPY
I decipher broken-boned sigmas
Split spheres and known symbols
So walk by
Gastro, physio, ophthalmo something
All Greek to me
In the waiting room
Small traumas and dramas
Wheeled athletes, stoic mothers
Old men, hyped children
Through open windows eye-sized
Swabs of cotton wool
Buoyed in the oxygen
What is this?
The doctor shrugs
Spring
Nothing to worry about

Gibraltar Glory

From his rock, his Jebel, Tariq smote
The king's army, helped by local treachery
Or incompetence, and contemplated Spain's
Jagged sierras blocking off the north.
His raiding party down to nine or ten
Thousand men and his Arab master
Musa surely fretting back in Africa;
But glory powered Berber swords
And Allah's storm proved irresistible –
Wind behind him, zeal in the ranks,
Tariq headlong into territory unknown
Took Toledo, and all Andalusia.

Next year Musa came and had his servant
Flogged for such egregious cheek
But granted him to keep command
And push the Arab empire on to France.

Gratitude is fickler than the wind:
Damascus summoned both its champions home
To pay for savouring their lavish victory,
Tariq reassigned to household servitude,
Musa to exile, poverty. With an afterthought,
A delivered gift from the Khalif,
The head of the son left in charge in Toledo.

At Thebes

A year was the somnolence
Between the river's floods.
Beneficent, like them, dynasties
Would swell and burst and wash away;
The fat-wet Nile slurped towards the sand
Which, detesting water, rolled repelled
Away out over Africa. It never rains.
In the stony dunes above the Nile
The scarab feeds on camel turd
Yet Ramses' priests thought him divine:
Ramses who stood ten times life height,
In stone ten thousand times its weight,
Now lies in bits. A camel's back bore
Too much straw, perhaps, a beetle
Nosed away three grains of sand,
Provoked the thunder of those mighty tons.
The earth in Egypt rarely quakes,
It must have trembled then
At history's massive hiccup.

Outremer

Culture shock is social intercourse gone bad abroad
Tourists gag on squalor, new cuisine and crowds
Bewildered troops misvalue foreign parts and rape and raze;
It goes both ways. In 1915 Aussies wrecked
Haret el Wazzir as pox and prices ran amok:
Egypt handles crisscross armies, like the host
Of Louis IX, surrendering – so many so in fact
Hundreds were beheaded every day, until the King
Was ransomed, handsomely. Now dollar-laden tourists stroll
In Shagarat el Dor, just slightly ill at ease;
A semi-soldier, fists around two wooden blocks, accosts
Americans, who blanch and shuffle back, repelled. Piastres,
conscience-money, serve to keep the stumps at bay;
With doubling of its revenue the State might keep
Its war-torn heroes out of sight – as we do back at home.

Home, via Darwin

Official top-end disorientation
Reminiscent of a sheep-dip;
First up a pre-dawn landfall,
Woolshed-type terminal,
Wall-eyed new arrivals dressed
Down by bellying boy scout
Customs men in khaki shorts.
Car park acres
Prop a toppling circus of stars,
Orion cartwheeling
Head over heels down under.

Noonday corrugated copperscapes
Gibber round Mt Isa
Shimmering with fahrenheit;
Air-conditioned waterhole,
Breezy T-shirt voices, clumps of glasses.
Back on board an accidental miner
Lashed and screened from tourist class;
Mushroom nimbus,
Ansett lurches in hot potholes,
We nervously
Order scotch shock absorbers.

Cladding 1988

The final touch: the granite cladding
On the Great Parliament of Canberra, adding
Gloss and lustre to the pile. Dreamers build
This way since Chephren sheathed his middle
Pyramid of Giza, white limestone filled
The awkward steps, veneered the riddle.
So lace and frills bedeck a wedding
And veil the coming lust of bedding.
This is not just decoration
(See the armour on the back
Of tortoises whose colouration
Stands up well against attack);
Externals are a celebration
And sacrifice to what we lack.

The House is landscaped, chambers surging
Up from relaid lawns submerging
Offices where light gleams dulled;
One role of Form is to befuddle,
Eyes are tricked and minds are gulled.
Later pharaohs also huddle
Underground and all their splurging
Is Form, is lost, eternal purging.
Let Content have a nobler notion,
Prefer, to brick, a rough-hewn rock,
Not require such self-promotion,
Beware of tendencies to mock,
Weigh the word and weigh the motion,
Never have to watch the clock.

The flag on giant flagpole flapping
Drowns the sound of clichéd clapping,
Clashes of each different symbol.
Internalising one may mumble:
Had Ramses foresight he might tremble,
Anticipate the robbers' scramble,
The stab and then the bandage ripping,
First and finest asset-stripping.
None escape from such dissection,
Values stood upon their head:
The critic has the last inspection,
No Content ever left for dead.
Form deemed sometimes near perfection
Is honoured in its life instead.

Hunter Valley Camouflage

The green myth of faraway hills in Sunday school hymns
Fills the Middle Hunter,
Paddocks and vine-lined slopes,
Higgledy-neat Golf Club swathes and swards,
Prosperous groups move against the trees; forearms arc.
The town itself is camouflaged with dots of brown
Horses, rusting tin roofs and flat facades;
From the air you'd not spot
The beer bottles in the cemetery
(A four-iron slice, say, from the roadside tee)
Catholics and Protestants in back-to-back lots
Practically forgotten;
Some mad park planner responsible perhaps
For these few acres of dead-heart hinterland,
Grassless, graceless,
Plastered on the healthy Singleton skin.
Pioneering names and dates have rubbed away,
Later generations peer through the stones:
Four children under five serially side by side,
Lonely Irish ladies of great age,
Some puzzled Germans.
Broken glass, few feeble weeds, slab on slab,
A sudden shock of fresh-placed flowers
For a daughter drowned now thirty years ago,
These the single colours in the place.

SS at Adelong

We fix fascist-murderer searchlights
On the cabin, to interrogate curfew-breakers:
A silly image this, like the clodhopper
Stopped glass-eyed in our glare
Blasted, hacked with a sticky black axe
Hunks tossed in the truck for the station dogs;
We heave homeward over front paddock.

Before breakfast mein host has other pests
Telephoto magnified posing on hummocks,
A live flop-eared soft toy sniffing
One good jump ahead of the trigger;
Later plastic bottles on a post
Better my aim, show the sights do need adjusting,
So we'll go back to that ghetto tomorrow.

The Crow and the Baby

Harsh drawled bird call without consonants asks
What point there is, condemns all truth as trite,
As irony: experience comes too late.

Crap, claptrap, shrieks the infant king, see
The given world is rearrangeable, so might
Is wrong, may will, and winners hesitate.

Family of crows like black sheep baa
With pecked-out eyes, spare themselves the sight
Of drought ahead dead certainly laid down by fate.

Off with their heads! And four and twenty tasks
Are to be jumped to, bottles, clothes and pies await
The hopeful yells of short-fused gelignite.

Soft ground sets under me like quick cement, turns cold,
A car starts cursing, other sounds drown out debate.
The sun of a sudden comes up in the campsite.

March 1918: Orders to his Men

1. This position will be held, and the section
      will remain here until relieved.

Some crazed janissary might so command
To hold the untenable, but for what end?
What programme might he have in mind?

2. The enemy cannot be allowed to interfere with this programme.

3. If the section cannot remain here alive
      it will remain here dead,
         but in any case it will remain here.

Glow-eyed youths marvellously alive
Race stooping on the slope
And yaw in death; yesterday's
Clawed figures on the wire.
Tomorrow pounces on the eye-blink now.
All the tenses stare together now.

4. Should any man, through shellshock or other cause,
      attempt to surrender, he will remain here dead.

I surrender to my own command
The double jeopardy of every contradiction.
I am a local God. All few of us,
The living dead, grin at my, at our apotheosis.

5. Should all guns be blown out the section
      will use Mills grenades and other novelties.

God of black winters
And presumably seasonal cycles of peace
Bring evolution, that time not so indecently be held.

6. Finally, the position as stated will be held.

The six orders, written in pencil, are in the Australian War Memorial,
Canberra. The lieutenant who wrote them was a clergyman before the war.
The position was held, until relieved.

King's Revenge

Do you recall years back
Crazy near Wonju high
On the steep deep-pile grass
Tumulus of King Sejong
Doing forward rolls?
First tight as a fist then
Pulled open by the slope
Stretched into looping dives
Rabbit-punching our vertebrae
Over and over. The king must
Have jerked his neck in his grave,
Demanded tribute; history
Somersaults, you never know
Comeuppance, scowl now
Under the gyrating catscanner,
At the subsequent cross-sections,
As life-size stone courtiers
Did at the lèse-majesté.

Peeking

China is changing too much for your liking?
A modern Ming golf course in planned for the Tombs,
Look, cranes make great letters that litter the skyline,
Mush of Hilton and Sheraton rooms.
What do you think of the leaden lid lifting?
Forbidden things curve as eaves in the air;
Serge is outmoded, no longer loose-fitting,
You see shaped bums now in Tienanmen Square.
Old-style, white-bloused girls at the Beijing Hotel
Guard a glass counter where foreigners buy
While utilitarian plush crimsons fade:
Silks, lacquer, strange roots, bottled non-ageing spell;
One hitches a stocking quite high on the thigh –
You surge, as light glancing on evergreen jade.

Winding-load Mode

Tokyo T-shirts
blurt slogans
codes, ads, odes
by the boobful
chesty headlines
weird wordings
synecdoches
picked from a dictionary
in my language
which I mind,

in two minds.

Reckon buggerit
and goodon'em.

Delayed at Narita,
I ponder the error
of not buying that one
designed phrase
to wear in those moments
of grinding repose
when I'm in the mode.

Trial and Error

'Soirée of avant-garde Japanese chamber music'
All manner of contradictions promised here
Open air with creaking wooden seats, floppy-
Shirted citizens, hot
Geraniums in flowerboxes
Tuning themselves.
Grand Yamaha pianoforte, doll-like pianist
Plunging on the extremities, and once or twice
Into the works;
Bamboo shakahaji sucked and blown
Puffed syllables exotically pronounced
A harp plucked, belled and beaten,
What's going on?

We put two big rocks,
Japanese-style, in our yard
Deliberately; one mossed and bossy
Shapeless, like half-heard haikus
On a cramjam train, irregular
As nature; the other tall, a dolmen,
Contemplative, alphabetical,
January through December.
Tribute to a logical tradition.
Gravid rain ran down them both
Differently.

I try things double-mindedly
Err maybe orientally

Crossing

Sometimes dusk-killed colours rise again and flare
Briefly for the skyline's passage into night,
A parable perhaps of gorgeous death with light
A miracle at last. It used to be that prayer
At bedtime guaranteed the journey on from there:
Hand to forehead, breast, in pious fright;
Then sleeping sicknesses and hazards out of sight
Like germs, like faith, like madness transited the air.
Eyes close. Red Sea waters in our minds divide
Historians interpreting remark the tide
Explanations blow along Great Bitter Lake;
In dreams the chronically irresolute decide
Bridge-burnt ventures thirty miles wide
Dunkirk's still-staggered morning-after pilots wake.

The Garden Path

Man standing
Dangle-hand Dad
Palm cupped up-
Side down buffs
Fair fuzzy
Feeling hair
Path sword on end
Cuts two lawns to
Yellow door
Stuck in bricks
Chimney puffs
Fluffy clouds
Mum at a window
Toe stub shoe stump
Door steps open
Jump a jump home
'Did you have a good time, eh?'
Smile for her
'Not yet'
Grown-ups stare sideways
Lean forward laughing

Vulgar and Vain Fractions

Thumbs drumming
Gashed wood desk top
Knife blades splay
He couldn't count for nuts
Fractions were worst
Chopped up ugly numbers
Would use his fingers
Trace hearts, initials
Slice one in half why not
Properly for a
Tenth, one over nineteen

But he was finicky
Scour back a written page
For uncurled ells
Any ems missing legs
Fret about spots, buttons,
Fingernails, dandruff
Was this womanish?

She took her eyes off
Traffic for a fraction
Mirror-tamping a curl
Kids skid dinking whip
Lash headon windscreens
Vanity out of all proportion

Some things like wheels
And bodies absolutely
Have to be perfect
This he can understand

Reaches down fingering
Each wheel rim
Propelling him
Paradoxically
Backwards.

Anachronisms

Black doodles score the phonebook
Graven nerves from June-July
Bad connections hum and garble
In each ear and hollow eye
Unplug me in the bathroom
Silver faces mouthing why
I should see you now.

The new girl soothes like unguents
And I hallow her today
Her amber and her marble
But anachronisms play
Like hands. You used to flinch
At fingertouch. I pushed, you slipped away
But I feel you now.

Improbability

It is PROBABLE that this or that
It is PROBABLE another thing
It is PROBABLE the theories
Babble on. Our science teacher
Knows he drones so scribbles
Oratorically but I stop slabbed
Against the bolder print which
Blobs and blubs like all the tests
We ever did with gas in glass retorts;
Molybdenum and plumbic lead
Aren't probable but do have poetry
In plosive liquid consonants.
Steele, are you here or somewhere else –
Perhaps you'll tell the class...
The droner interrupts and rubs
His board, my smile gone with
Chalk and all that alchemy;
Sudden problems sneer insoluble.

Or

North-south, black-white must separate
Are split with and or or
Subjects have their predicate
It's never clear what for
Picoseconds calculate
Which switch is off or on
Then as our facts accelerate
Are they here or gone

Psychologists like yes-no tests
No answer is 'correct'
But pattern-forming manifests
So selves can be cross-checked
And politicians opt in twos
Whole mandates we elect
By simple votes and people lose
When plebiscites reject

It's we who seek polarity
No real reason why we should
For Deists, singularity
Encapsulates the All and Good
And nature says with clarity
There's east and west and realms between
And space beyond: disparity
That artifices leave unseen

No Smell Museum

Before embalming
Pharaoh's brains were hooked on wire
Unbundled through the nose:
Choice thoughts twitch in the Egyptian section.
You turn and pull a face that's
Held in glass cases;
In stale, tomby conditioning of air
One stone scarab bends so smoothly
Rubbable.

Outside, red double-decker hubbub dubbed
On tapes that play, replay
For me the sounds and sights of us
Collected with a single mind and
Catalogued.

From the hotdog stand
You come at me with verbs and vowels
As shooed pigeons
Frittering
Against grey buildings
Peel stalely away;
You say exhaling, '
Onion paragraph dabbed with
Cologne

Alone and dozing different senses
Can be trundled through the head
And logged: not smell.
Their flat-stacked histories
Fill museums; but scent ungathered
Never might have been
Like mumbled words, quick kisses, idle thoughts,
Instead this is the here and now, the being
Hooked.

Of Parabolas and Parables

Speck of black on blue
Arcs slow, stops, drops perpendicular,
The y-line of its graph,
An eagle on a kitten.
Geometric goddish death
Like this should come to us
The to-be-smitten.

Dot is blown into a globe
So poets, preachers, artists generalise
Axis of each eye particular
Tangential wheeling
Souls in Paradise are skylark
Spirits pencilled curve suggests a
Bird of feeling.

Sower's arm extends in seed
In falling dots to goodish ground;
Sparrow frailly turns its skull
To curving cat, and all of us are bitten.
Horror later fades: vernacular
Sermons, poems and equations draw out fate
The to-be-written.

Suspension

Plane hangs
Ambiguous
Giotto flat out on a fresco
Yearns for perspective
Space layered, foreshortened
Palest sky plaster
Sungold disk sparkles
Flying halo
I grunt
Staccato disbelief;
Characters in novels converse oratorically,
Actors elocute rounded considerations
Better than real, straighter than lines,
Picasso
Blurts disjunctions.

Boeing bounds down the tarmac
Heat haze shimmering dimensions.

Looking-glass Jungle

The Fly:
Grandscale maps of Papua and photos from space
sprawl flat on the page; but the bow-wave
writhes round coiled corners ahead
to the tail-whipped fork-tongue coast.

River's face-down sameness like
tarot card backs hiding paranoias
smothered on green beize;
dome of brain-grey air, veils of rain.
The water wraps its blindfold and lies
about logs, snouts, underworld rhythms,
a tease of negatives and absences –
nothing is sure, made, right angled.

The Alice:
Hemmed giant vegetating dalliance,
great sage dames and jade marchionesses
parade on stage, ribbons festooning,
pendants and shawls; huge emerald noblemen
jostle minions, collapsing tree curtains.
Scenes swivel, an outboard motor coughs, the court
stares: from the wings an impromptu canoe,
crew in pants and shirts quick and silent,
exits incongruous.

Sun splinters the looking-glass clouds
like a bedroom awaking.
A white china egret rises from the mantelpiece.

The rivers meet.

Real Time

Then they were prosperous
Plus-foured and jodhpured
Posing in sepia
Groups, moustaches and parasols
News crepitated via
Cloth-fronted wirelesses
Grandchildren bowling hoops
Flat-nosed at sweet stores
Airplanes were gimcracked
Loops looped quite silent
Crick-necked observers aahed
In slow motion

Free time now marketed
Incomes disposable
Plastics and gimmickry
Leisure in living rooms
Audio video
Kids with controls in hand
Stare at black windows
Printing out phosphorous
Data, looped programs
Space simulations
Quick-reflexed participants
Slip to the future, click
Instant replays

Ancientest Power

He'd rid himself of underlings unconscionably –
This one displeases me, and this –
Not reckon orphaning and laying waste to dreams.
An hour or so from now a hall will graft
To his words, poise to applaud
Announcement of further usurpations.
Power redefines itself at altitude,
A common, queenly smile has hold of him,
Mocks all indulgences available.
He waits for her return, but schemes collapse,
Words fail. He is unmanned. Another smile:
Please do up your seatbelt, sir.

You Like a Good Murder

I like a good murder
Splashed red in the newspaper
Some knotted family cut with a kitchen knife
Bits and pieces by Agatha Christie
Ask yourself why
Outrage, mind-fire
A type of desire
I, you, mathematically
Cubed and rooted in rooms
Social decimals
Behind bars like equal-signs
And the night thrills between.

Your honour, look at you
Drool at the details
You are my client
Some of this blood
Too, is yours.

Don't Overegg

Don't overegg the pudding, said the judge:
Counsel nodded, wishing now he'd been less rich.
Pale, his client whisks the offending phrases.

Vegans never overegg: but their extremes
Risk blandness, cutting down good foods.

Enthusiasts of all kinds egg on. And err.

Don't over anything. The Eiger climbers
Ledged and grappling through binoculars
Think of Humpty Dumpty and the jokey rocks
Below – Brandegg, Honegg, Eggblatz.

Nursery words wag caveats
To be ignored that is
If kids will ever reach the peaks.

Pilate's Question

They say that pig fat made the sepoys mutiny:
I say they say since victors smear the facts of history
Notoriously. Things set solid yesterday
Elasticate when told in court by witnesses;
Conviction hangs on tricks of advocates,
Not to mention simple jurymen's credulity.
It's how you come across – this politicoes,
Groomed for success with manicure and maquillage,
Know well. Words convey much less in interviews
Than body signs. Words do have power, though, for whispering,
In innuendo, rumour-form, out-shouts the gospel truth.
Well may you ask yourself what evidence
Is unequivocal.

It Can't Happen to Me

Jostling lab rats scoot today
Careless round their Nurburgring and
Free until the experimenting hand
Drops down selectively so that we may
In twos mesh our cogs unpenalised, gland
And hips interconnected connive
To surge the virus and drive
Like the clappers perhaps to expand
Commuter odds of nine to five
On the orbital, a steering pin gives way
And ambulances' unmelodic sirens play
Luring spectators in yonderness meaning I've
Yet again proved quite conclusively
That it did not happen to me

The Last

The last great Western martyrdom
was probably in Otranto
which the Ottomans besieged
and gave the 800 holders-out
the choice to change belief.

No deal: they stepped forward
to be decapitated one by one
on an August afternoon.

Showcased cluttering behind glass
in the duomo's farthest reach
are all the massed skulls,
plus some ornamental bones.

I reflect, while mirrored eyes
waver in the sockets:
yes, zeal perhaps at first,
but for the queuing last
wouldn't futility, pragmatism,
God's presumed mercy
justify declining?

Modern heads nod:
too odd for words anybody
would opt for the axe.

Afterwards the executioner,
by such witnessed faith converted,
was also put to death.